My God Appears

JEFFREY JUBELIRER

Inquiries and Book Orders should be addressed to:

Great Writers Media
Email: info@greatwritersmedia.com
Phone: (302) 918-5570

ISBN: 978-1-960939-36-4 (sc)
ISBN: 978-1-960939-37-1 (ebk)

Contents

. . . .

Happy Passover and Happy Easter! Jeffrey
is a jew for Jesus, the Christ.

Jeffrey D. Jubelirer has lived through many religious practices with hope to be alive and well. Thankful for the gifts of life and love, he has been writing for more than 50 years since his days at University Of Pennsylvania and Duquesne University.

As this is an introduction and comments for this book called My God Appears By Jeffrey David Jubelirer.

I will like to make certain comments and tell and make of shown that this book is both religious and spiritual and written with great brevity as Jeff says so very much in such few words as a famous Author Only and Poet. That is the category that us Authors, Writers and Poets have now reached. He has many, many finished writings and books. He just does now have 12 books. He has more books than Ernest Hemingway and he has friends who were telling him that he is comparable to Ernest Hemingway.

We do like to mention the book, The Sun Also Rises together.

Jeff is compassionate and very kind and a very decent man and human being with accolades that of the Holy Scriptures, that he is truly one Hebrew King. He does like to give back whenever he can. He always makes my day whenever we have been together of our life on in God Almighty. We both walk the walk and talk the talk of prayers and scripture readings and coming to places of public worship whenever such events are available to us.

Hope you like the book here!

Very Truly Yours,
SherAnne Shea Jubelirer

To my acquaint, whom I have had the priviledge to serve.

Mr. Jeffrey Jubelirer- a poet who reaches the world.

Jean G. Moore, M.A.
July 27, 2018

Reign Or Shine

. . . .

The reign of God is at hand
But does the world understand
Although I think they do
No one will surely know
Until the time that God comes to command
Then we will surely know for
The door is open
And we had come thru thanksgivingl

By Jeffrey D. Jubelirer, commentary from Steven Michael Shea
And Fixed and Edited By SherAnne Shea Jubelirer

As We Stand For God!

. . . .

As I stand on top of the bridge
Never wanting a fire
Or a burn.
They are swimming
And the sign means nothing.
Forgiveness
And simple
Joy
Fun for all.
White doves coming
Closer
Climbing up out of the stream
And wishing
A Happy Father's Day!

By Jeffrey D. Jubelirer

Inspired By Gay Kelly, My Therapist

· ·

Time goes fast
One day at a time
And sometimes with you.
We are bringing order
From chaos with help
And management
Therapy and accepting
The love and words
And giving up seeking power
But true power coming
From somewhere
Perhaps known as God.
He has loved me
And I might be different
Or out of the ordinary.
Weird and odd are words that hurt me.

By Jeffrey D. Jubelirer

Theory Of A Love

. . . .

The word "apart" is not needed
To be heard
Silence is easier handled
With same power past a step
And control in my life.
My heart is tender
I get hurt easily
Fickle person or am I the stupid person
Who needs to understand?
Coming running
Avoiding the hurt
Staying away
And not reacting quickly
With out thought
Sober with vigilance
I overcome fears to live and love.
And have careful gratitude
Resolving alone with my God.

By Jeffrey.

Hold Me Tonight Forever

. . . .

Hold me tonight forever
Growing love sensitizes
Of that being and giving me the strength
To continue.
My Lord and our Lord
Your Lord with us
Continuing to grow in fellowship
Works for love
Wanted for sharing in our lives
A place to teach each other
And help
DEVELOP more respect and honor
For hopes for all of us.

By Jeffrey D. Jubelirer

Rare Am I Living

. . . .

Maybe on the other side
Close for redemption
Structures in freedom,
I give away too to live alive
And waiting loved reactions.
Care does go close to trees
Past the inkwell long to be.
Now the hunger for needs
Place inside aside to write for someone.
All calling to see needing
And looking far across the city,
For there is plenty of truth
And peace paused resting with the Catholic Church and God Almighty.
And making prayers,
Slowly making a sanctuary, driven
Walking quickly,
Thru darkness to light,
Flames.
Eyes thankful.

Wake, rare I am living all for time
Consumed to try to listen
And learn even more of the Truth.
Sherry says the truth is her light
From a quote of a Latin proverb.

By Jeffrey D. Jubelirer

A Climb

. . . .

Rising to resurrection love
Eternal days above
Close to heaven
We sing and do believe
A search is found
As sound creation of forgiveness.
We recognize You True
Rising thru resurrection love
Climbing steps to a Kingdom Of God.

By Jeffrey D. Jubelirer

Breath Of God

. . . .

Our dads do love us
And the Supreme Father gives us life:
Movement, exercise, warmth of day
Tree of night time
And brains reflect, reorganize and create
To arrange choices
Roses blossom
Water flows for free somewheres'
Flowing free to homes and people
Maybe with love.
God is alive
The wind keeps giving energy
We know little the beginning breath.

By Jeffrey D. Jubellrer

Ready

. . . .

The night brought waves white
Smoothe, so smoothe
Another day at the beach gone
And worn another day alive with God.
Almost sad to find the ticket returning home.
We sat at benchs alive
And music playing overhead to try
To drown the sorrow of returning to the city in the big overgrown
bus.
I lost a little money I could have bought
A week's worth of groceries with
But I felt healthy and In love with life, I was
Almost ready for tomorrow.

By Jeffrey D. Jubelirer

Let Me

. . . .

Dear Lord Jesus
Let me humble my haughty eyes
Let me run away from the evil I have entered
Let me choose your peace
Let me cross the barrier
And let me illuminate my spirit, with your discipline.

O drink my blood
And freshen me with yours
Give me the foundation to walk in pleasure of your companionship.
Give me the son
Take away the torture of being without a God.

By Jeffrey D. Jubelirer

So Hurt

I am so hurt inside
I am less loved than needed
And hurt so deep.
Was it the difference or the disease?
Why was I powerless
Why didn't I listen
And stop the running after people, places and things?
But I am at a meeting now
Hoping, trying not to expect
And willing to learn more
Thanks
God for awakening me.

By Jeffrey D. Jubelirer

Positive Sight

. . . .

And I pray with awareness
A hope comes to play.
A positive sight of the nature
And the sun's ray
The sky's
And the seeds developing peace
By the water of God beginning,
The beginning of infinity
And hopefully continues.

By Jeffrey D. Jubelirer

Dear Holy Father in Heaven,

. . . .

Bless our home
Let it be filled with Saints
And righteous living.
Bless our hearts that they be pure
And filled with your love.
Bless our minds that they be honored
Of your presence.
Thank you Jesus, our friend
Our body, our soul,
Our spirit, our friend,
Our guiding light.

By Jeffrey D. Jubelirer

I Am Ready

. . . .

I am ready to understand and study
The words-changes and more,
Bright romantic moons,
Walking and talking
The Holy Spirit keeps me busy,
And poetry and love
Of nature.
Bond the place
Even the moment I open my eyes
To relay a message of hope
Care and warmth go wherever
And from day to day.
Love and work and always
The ground and the sky
To be and see feelings all of it.

By Jeffrey D. Jubelirer

Struggle Or Pleasure

. . . .

Glad to bring principles honest enough
And toughened up to the outside
And again and again.
Another time for music
For vacation time from work,
Struggle or pleasure
Driven to come out on firm ground.
Importance, worthy statements
And poetry working on me
And all listening to be children of God
Where we go and what calls
From term to term.
We have smiled for future wellness.
Conquerors and maybe masters loving
All the Way, deep.

By Jeffrey D. Jubellrer

We Learn Everyday

. . . .

So sweetly speaking to you
O Lord
We talk to each other now.
Red lights,
Soothing words
And tunes
Perpetuate of desire
And perfection possible,
Judge
As a handsome reward
To your children
Trying
And allowing hearts to love and feel.

Can we laugh together
At the end of the world
Infinity also?

I like and feel heavenly;
Its all right
God said so on the seventh
Day God rested,
Moments and days
Going and coming.

Life Changes

. . . .

We are all petals of all flowers
Growing together in hopes of love.
Each one expressive
Till the completion of the garden
Welcomes and is alive graciously smiling.
Really.
Though often sweated for
The ground solidly remains
Though changes
And is cleaned.

By Jeffrey D. Jubelirer

Dear God

. . . .

And I feel a quick
Burden removed
I don't bother myself
And nature sets me free.

By Jeffrey D. Jubelirer

I Took the Time

. . . .

Thank you Lord
I took the time to love
You told me to share and give what I can be
Doing and praying
Silence and speech
Music still playing
Trying to stop smoking
Singing for more breath
Till a better tomorrow
Already agreeing with Madonna or Venus
In the forest great as the stars that will shine.

By Jeffrey D. Jubelirer

Dear Adonoi Eloheem

. . . .

Pleasure to greet you
Pleasure to meet you
Creator of my freedom
Out of Egypt
And out of tyranny years.
Later,
I am thankful
And proud
To praise and love.
I am thankful to speak
And hear.
Thank you, Almighty God

Religious, Loving God
By Jeffrey D. Jubelirer

Feeling a Peace

. . . .

On the seashore
At the seashore
I climbed to the breaker of the waves.
The beach, the sea gulls crying out
Popcorn on top of sand castles
The sun came out
And we walked for miles,
Clam shells to be stepped
I cracked them.
She took off her shoes and ran.
I stood and felt the breeze
She ran a way.
Seeing her for miles
Looking up and feeling the never
Ending
Feeling a peace of mind.
The ocean waves flowing home to us,
Alive
Creating a space for time's love
Everlasting I go back to the machines.
No need to talk,
God was speaking.

By Jeffrey D. Jubelirer

I Seek

. . . .

Be more and/or be enough.
To be good to oneself
Is God's Love.
And do I understand
Constant Messiah work in life
Or am I one of many
Who want to complete the program
Of our lives?
I see thee Eternal.

By Jeffrey D. Jubelirer

I Say

The Sacred Heart makes me pray
I say I receive Holy Spirit
Talking to me
Dear One
Mention the Lord.
My tears have sparkled
To my heart
I pray to be holy and honorable.

By Jeffrey D. Jubelirer

I Ask

. . . .

Holy Father in heaven
I back the truth in answering
All the hope I can receive
So I relish in life
And dedicate myself
To you eternally as I worship
And require and need
Your King Jesus in my heart.
All around me there is weakness
And dispute.
Yet, I ask you for your love.

By Jeffrey D. Jubelirer

Heavenly Attitudes Come

My friends touched me
Last night;
My mask came off
Darkness allowed.
The stars shine
While we hold hands
On our way to morning.
The walk to the chapel
Building from one rock
In the center of the earth, we cherish.
We laugh,
We love
And thank God
Giving us our lives
With heavenly hope
Beyond the tears
And work.
We now enjoy till always
And everlasting.
Heavenly attitudes come.

By Jeffrey D. Jubeltrer

Take My Hand

. . . .

Dandy, I am
you chose me
literally
make me talk
feature of the rock
sing this thing I grasp.
Importance
forgiveness
growth to rest
and further on
the Kingdom Of God.

By Jeffrey D. Jubelirer

Learning About God

. . . .

Often I feel so fulfilled
and comfortably relaxed
to learn
open to better days
and awareness.

I am trying to sit still.

The speaker asked God
for help.

I followed her suggestion.

By Jeffrey D. Jubelirer

And Maybe Tomorrow

. . . .

A smile
A look
A careful transaction
Perpetuation of good and a warm hello
Hoping of truth and honor
And maybe tomorrow.

By Jeffrey D. Jubelirer

Just Me

. . . .

In the beginning
Opens infinity
The grace of God
Sometimes to see up
And get close,
Sometimes poets speak real words.

Every time seeing you
The wind is adventure
And hearing you comes the inspirations completely,
Chosen to much for me-
Just me.

By Jeffrey D. Jubelirer

July 24, 2008

. . . .

We saw in time
Climb the heritage
Sing a song
strong memories fill
The air
And care for heaven
Still on earth
Will I beckon alive
Dive into the depths
And reach for all above.
Love is good and more
To ask and give
We live today.

By Jeffrey D. Jubelirer

January 4, 2007

. . . .

My talk
Our walk
We do more
The core of the apple
Soothe my heart
I think better
Each day
Watching the sun.
Come
And hide
For rest.
Test of our hearts
Cruising to learn.

By Jeffrey D. Jubelirer

We All Come To A Peace

. . . .

Everyone all call over.
I am helpless over all people I was told;
And I believed I could give love
To just say hi.

Practicing on learning my manhood
And saying godliness and spiritual awakenings
The ability own a oneness
Humbly hoping a presence of Creator.
Sensitive to good
And hurting of bad;
Conscience and judgement are necessary
For survival today.
We all come to a place
The unity of same and unique.

By Jeffrey D. Jubelirer

Growing Closer

Two or three
Even more there are
We too can be
Two radically powering a change
A messianic forest where
God and we share beauty.
Only one man
Only
One higher power
Pumping gas
Pumping the blood
To the brain
Covered or consecrated.
Loser or winner
Equal moments for society
Composing the symphony to play
Listening and growing closer.

By Jeffrey D. Jubelirer

Talking About Life

....

There is a breeze out tonight, I fight
But I have succumbed,
Thank you God.
I was accepted in trinity mystery
The Son's family
I was taught
"One God before me."
We are equal people
Some might say
That money talks.
Jesus was poor and slept anywhere.
Is everyone a son to someone?
God blesses America!
How we are so blest!

By Jeffrey D. Jubelirer

The Gate

· ·

Teaming up with me
And a thanks for most of me
Day or night.
I fly high, sober for you and your most
I rely on my God.
Discussing, praying and doing
Our eyes gleaming
The light of day
And our souls were home.
Together is our favorite word.
Working till I heard.
Going further and arising
Days are ready for us to sing and to fly
I can see the fountain of love and youth.
Perhaps right and now forever
We push the gate.

By Jeffrey D. Jubellrer

Tasting

. . . .

Ah! The taste of a good cup of coffee
Tasting strong
Feel peace and stand to dance with the crying
Fading a way and I praise the Lord,
True love.
I express and relax and thank God
Through my Lord
He promises I won't perish
So I sleep better and have positive energy.

By Jeffrey D. Jubelirer

And Believed

. . . .

A great pleasure
In this world
My places
Reach the moment.
Giving a smile with warmth
And pleasure gives
Someone near, close
And believed
To be heavenly touched.

By Jeffrey D. Jubelirer

Dear God

. . . .

And Mother nature be,
And I singular or plural
Rest
And arise
To your temple
Of a holy nation.
Of priests and Rabbis
Above the call chooses to be a right light,
Summary is intact!

By Jeffrey D. Jubelirer

To Care And Love

. . . .

Unique moments
Come on else where without me.
Am I certain all alone
And yet close to prayer.
Redeeming within the sour bread
Spoiled and mean.
I walk where to go and show
I will look down with my heart pumping life
And then all the Way up.
Angels and people
Questions and answers pure to be best
Senses used
And cleansing the soul forever.
Worshipping and loving to try,
To care and love.

By Jeffrey D. Jubelirer

Amen, Amen

. . . .

Teach me something I must learn
The focus is on the strength
To pure and beneficent
To loving and cleanness.
To talk to God and be understood
To be alone and sing
To be alone and be in awe
True love favors willingness.

By Jeffrey D. Jubelirer

Appreciation

· ·

Sunshine
Rhymes my rhythm
You teach me someone today
I can care.
Energy feels
Grows and carries
Fulfillment of love where
How and why.
The cunning ability
With pockets of bread
Talks to God
A sincere thank you.
Given life and time
To think and to run
And walk with spirit,
Consideration and appreciation
Really needs to be appreciated.

By Jeffrey D. Jubelirer

Quietly

. . . .

Righteous be seeking as long as can be
Rejoicing and even more
Quietly
Worship real life.
We can learn from all
And help sanctify the world with compassion and humility
Recognize goodness with judgement as God wishes
To serve the living creation
Welcome for all days of life.
Blessings to be read and deeply understood.
The heart and mind to sanity and development
To be understood enough
To be forever for God Almighty.

By Jeffrey D. Jubelirer

I Am Aware

. . . .

Champions walk tall
And are the first to bow.
Look, see the American flag
Calling out to the seas.
Guided by the eyes only given to the One.
Congratulations mean so much
But fists hard
Can be softened, so quickly
With a kind word.
To realize passages and arrivals through out
And time wakes to recognize God who has shown us up.

By Jeffrey D. Jubelirer

August 7, 1995

. . . .

I am not desperate
I am happy
Even moments of stillness cross my path.
The soul consistent
Or constant
And here where we start
The new step
Rises from sleep.
Resurrected till tomorrow
Now here
Where we are
A light to life
And we love.

By Jeffrey D. Jubelirer

Still Bright

. . . .

Oh injured soul stays alive!
Come up again and bring hope of love
Though tougher now real and accepting
Still bright and seeking the steps in order.
Endless to love true softening and gentle,
Genuine
Straight for the light
Chances take
Life in awe
For happiness or joy, Lord watching.
Which one guides and directs all
And future understanding for more.

By Jeffrey D. Jubelirer, a jew.

December 29, 1995

. . . .

The fence outside the gate
Territory to be gained
Territory to be cherished.
Birth rates of goodness
Arise
And hope for the future.
Thank God for God
Holding my hand
Or am I delusional?

To think of happiness
And joy tomorrow
Are good
And definitely positive!

Cultural Council November 27, 1996
By Jeffrey D. Jubelirer

With the Light

· ·

And I can see love
Growing we do
More energy and time for each one
We together make
The seasons get better
Our stories live
And we receive giving
Today is lasting
Hold on for hope
Our faith develops our trust
More than ever felt.
Tomorrow soon comes
Waking and rested for more to see
Your tender moments I grasp
Sensitive and more
You are dancing and singing for the Lord,
I am standing beside.

By Jeffrey D. Jubelirer

Born Again

. . . .

Hungry feeling for day, in addition,
The night time takes me up
All around to within serious moments.
To carry me to Hollywood and Nashville.
Needing a little affection, can I survive
And maybe serve to be served.
The expectations should lovingly go away
To a man, a human being
Sometimes tender, gentle
I hope that firm is principle when needed.
I grow into the man with a plan.
I grow into the creation
Awake and directed
Calling out
Licensed and certified
For integrity and honor,
Born again.

By Jeffrey D. Jubelirer

March 5, 2007

· ·

Tonight light
Brings hope
And raisins of fruit always better,
The bitter almost past.

By Jeffrey D. Jubelirer

The Messiah Comes

· ·

I was frightened
Maybe too much tomorrow.
The license states
I can say no.
I can give with a generous heart
Whatever I have to give.
Do you know today?
I am tense this moment.
Can I keep same myself?
There is equality
That I am told
The Messiah comes
And I must relax
And let go forward speaking.

By Jeffrey D. Jubelirer

www.ingramcontent.com/pod-product-compliance
Lightning Source LLC
Chambersburg PA
CBHW070942120626
46546CB00004B/1521